THE ANCIENT PICTS OF THE SCOTTISH HIGHLANDS OF THE SEVENTH CENTURY

THE ANCIENT PICTS OF THE SCOTTISH HIGHLANDS OF THE SEVENTH CENTURY

Michael Sheane

ARTHUR H. STOCKWELL LTD
Torrs Park, Ilfracombe, Devon, EX34 8BA
Established 1898
www.ahstockwell.co.uk

British Library Cataloguing-in-Publication Data.
A catalogue record for this book is available
from the British Library.

Arthur H. Stockwell Ltd bears no responsibility
for the accuracy of information recorded in this book.

ISBN 978-0-7223-5142-0
Printed in Great Britain by
Arthur H. Stockwell Ltd
Torrs Park   Ilfracombe
Devon EX34 8BA

By the same author:

Ulster & Its Future After the Troubles (1977)
Ulster & The German Solution (1978)
Ulster & The British Connection (1979)
Ulster & The Lords of the North (1980)
Ulster & The Middle Ages (1982)
Ulster & St Patrick (1984)
The Twilight Pagans (1990)
Enemy of England (1991)
The Great Siege (2002)
Ulster in the Age of Saint Comgall of Bangor (2004)
Ulster Blood (2005)
King William's Victory (2006)
Ulster Stock (2007)
Famine in the Land of Ulster (2008)
Pre-Christian Ulster (2009)
The Glens of Antrim (2010)
Ulster Women – A Short History (2010)
The Invasion of Ulster (2010)
Ulster in the Viking Age (2011)
Ulster in the Eighteenth Century (2011)
Ulster in the History of Ireland (2012)
Rathlin Island (2013)
Saint Patrick's Missionary Journeys in Ireland (2015)
The Story of Carrickfergus (2015)
Ireland's Holy Places (2016)
The Conqueror of the North (2017)
The Story of Holywell Hospital: A Country Asylum (2018)
Patrick: A Saint for All Seasons (2019)
The Picts: The Painted People (2019)
Pictland: The Conversion to Christianity of a Pagan Race (2020)
Irish & Scottish Dalriada (2020)
The Roman Empire (2021)

CHAPTER ONE

By the early seventh century the ancient Picts of the Scottish Highlands were turning away from paganism to embrace the religion of the Church of Rome. After 600 the historical sources become more reliable. The list of Pictish kings is the basic chronological guide, but other sources cite Bede, Adomnan and the Irish annalists. The sixth century had ended with a man called Nechtan as paramount ruler of the Picts. Much academic conjecture surrounds him. Whether he was a Pict or a Briton is unknown for sure.

Dumbarton Castle has been pointed to as a residence of the Pictish kings. Dumbarton means the Fort of the Britons – Dun Breatann. A poem also relates to a later king of the Picts who defeated the Northumbrian English in 685. One Beli married a Pictish princess, and the child of the union was the Pictish King Brude. In the Clyde genealogy the father of Beli appears as Nechtan, son of Cano, whose death in 621 is recorded in the Irish annals. He was probably a Pict. Brude was one of the most powerful Pictish over-kings.

The Picts may now have ruled both their own kind and the Britons. The royal family of Alt Clut maintained dynastic control in Pictavia for at least two generations after 600. Now a dynasty of Britons wanted to seize control in Pictavia, but no surviving source cites the Picts as being ruled by any others in the seventh century.

Nechtan, King of the Picts, and Neithon, King of Alt Clut, were contemporaries and neighbours, but not the same man – such is the confusion in the annals. A dynasty of Britons was now seen to control much of Pictavia, and perhaps another force ruled the area of the Clyde. No surviving source implies that a Pictish king ruled the Picts and the Britons in the early seventh century. That two kings were reigning in Pictavia at the same time seems unlikely.

The reign of Nechtan, King of the Picts, witnessed several important political events. According to the king list he ruled for twenty years, from c.600 to c.620. This coincided with a period in which there was dynastic strife between two northern English kingdoms, each ruled by its own king. Out of this strife emerged the realm of Northumbria, meaning the lands north of the Humber.

The Bernician King Aethelfrith defeated the Scots army at the battle of Degasaran in 603, and expelled the reigning king to become the first ruler of all Northumbria. His enemies fled into exile among the Britons before finding an English protector.

In 617 a great battle in the Midlands paved the way for one Edwin's restoration; the victory was so decisive that Edwin gained the overlordship of Northumbria. Now it was the turn of the Bernician royal family to flee into exile, to find refuge in the Celtic north. Others fled to Scottish Dalriada, seeking refuge among the Scots. The eldest son fled to Pictavia, where he married a Pictish princess and fathered a son. Edwin perceived the political benefits of being a Christian, so he became a convert. He followed the religion of the Church of Rome, which had recently established itself among the southern English.

In the seventh century the Celtic churches were established in the northern and southern parts of Britain and in Ireland, where the Church took on a Gaelic character. Columba's Iona and its 'familia' of dependent monasteries in Argyll and Pictavia formed one group while Armagh in Ireland formed another. The Britons of Wales, Cornwall and the North were part of a third group. But Columba's Gaelic church was not separate from mainstream Roman Catholicism. These Celtic churches were remote geographically from Rome, so they tended to go their own way. Celtic churches retained an outmoded style of the tonsure, and celebrated Easter on a different day from that in the Church of Rome. Later in this essay it will be seen how these issues came to a crisis in the 660s, with far-reaching consequences for the Picts.

Now came the question of matrilineal succession, which involved the practice of fosterage. This meant more than giving shelter and protection; it was a political gesture of great significance in a blood bond sealed by oath and ritual. The Pictish king who gave hospitality to princes and other nobility may have wanted non-aggression treaties. The sources show many instances of inter-dynastic union, not all of which were marital, occurring all over the British Isles at that moment. This was a period in which written treaties were non-existent. The Picts seem to have employed inter-dynastic unions in a way that their neighbours did not.

Many historians believe that succession lay not through the male line, but through the female. Such a system is known as matriliny, whereby a king was not necessarily succeeded by his son. This practice was not widespread in the British Isles or indeed on the continent in any period of recorded history. Other societies worldwide have practised matrilineal succession – some African tribes had a matrilineal tradition. If the Picts practised matrilineal succession, it may have been restricted to royal succession and was not practised by the ordinary people. The earliest information on Pictish royal succession comes from Bede. In his remarks about British people, he says that the Picts originated in the near east and from there sailed westwards to the British Isles. They first landed in Ireland, but were repulsed by the Gaels, or Irish, who directed them to settle in Britain.

Matrilineal succession was known in Pictavia in Bede's lifetime. Bede observed that the Picts had no wives, but that they freely gave themselves up to what we would call free sex. No king was succeeded by his son until the nature of kingship began to enter a period of great change. However, there is no evidence that Pictish women held greater political power than their counterparts in Ireland, the Britons, Scots or English. Early historic society was quite patriarchal and rarely mentioned women in its records. Even high-status women are sometimes insignificant in the records and in society. The name of the dynastically important female is frequently forgotten in oral traditions of a matrilineal society. The Irish annals only record a few women whom we can identify as Picts.

A quarter of the rulers in the Pictish king list were succeeded by a brother, this being normal in a matrilineal system. Other close kin, such as cousins who shared a common grandmother, appear in the king list. Most kings in the king list have typical Pictish names drawn from a limited pool, but the names were not restricted to one family; they appear to have been used by a number of designated kindred whose representatives were eligible for the over-kingship of Pictavia. Popular names included Talcoran, Talcors, Nechtan and Gartmaits. Baby boys were earmarked as potential over-kings of Pictland and were given a suitably kingly name from the small selection available. Their mothers belonged to a wealthy group of royal families whose male offspring competed for power in some kind of formal king-making system, but how this system worked is not known.

It, however, allowed not only full-blooded Picts but also the sons of non-Pictish fathers and mothers to be given kingly names, and these sons were also eligible under the matriliny rules to be anointed kings of Pictavia. Some historians have suggested that men whose blood was only half Pictish were accepted as royal claimants through a policy of exogamous marriage – marriage outside the kindred. By this means, husbands for Pictish princesses were found not only outside the province or subkingdom, but frequently in foreign lands. Exogamy was perhaps the norm within Pictdom, and marriage alliances between Pictish royal families were no doubt common, but only two figures in the king list can be safely identified as the sons of foreign fathers. Sometimes kings went into exile, during which they fathered sons. One Beli ruled the Picts in the latter part of the seventh century; his offspring Brude also ruled the Picts in the latter part of this period, and he is one of the most renowned figures in the early historic age.

Two non-Pictish fathers in the king list were Domnall Brecc of Dalriada, who died in 643, and Maelgwn of Gwynedd. Dromnall Brecc was the grandson of Columba's royal patron. The Donuel of the king list may have been a Scot, a Briton or an Irishman – it was a common name in many parts of the British Isles in this period. Royal princes who sprang from non-Pictish fathers were almost certainly raised by the Picts. The young folk were perhaps kept close to their mother's kin, to be nurtured as candidates for the over-kingship.

Nothing in the sources indicates that these princes sought political advancement in their fathers' spheres; nor is there any indication of a parallel movement of non-Pictish princesses being acquired as wives for Pictish men. It may have been a precondition of an inter-dynastic marriage that a non-Pictish father took no part in his child's development and that he surrendered responsibility for these matters to the woman's family. These princes regarded themselves as Picts and spent their formative years in an entirely Pictish setting. Non-Pictish fathers who were of royal status in their own land were willing to acquiesce in this arrangement. If the 'marriage' was a permanent union formalised by ritual, a foreign king might expect economic and political benefits in exchange for his sons becoming breeding stock for future Pictish royalty. On the other hand, some coercion by the Pictish side may have been employed, especially if the foreign king and his son were already tributary to the Picts.

What then were the advantages of a matrilineal system? Why was it peculiar to the Picts and not others in the British Isles? First of all, more than one royal family could claim the over-kingship or high kingship. An over-king of Pictavia was the acknowledged ruler of a group of provinces or subkingdoms, but only one of them could be selected as the best contender. Intermarriage between these royal families, together with marriages involving Pictish princesses and non-Pictish men, created a varied pool of candidates. The process of selecting an over-king would therefore benefit from a matrilineal system, for the heir would be selected by quality rather than by birth. An ineffective son would not succeed his father; instead the brothers and nephews of the king would become eligible to succeed him, the best among them being selected. But the inheritance of property and status in Pictavia as a whole was probably from father to son, and only the over-king, the paramount ruler of the Picts, was succeeded by his brother or by his sister's son.

Some historians believe that Pictish royal succession was not matrilineal. They usually focus on Bede's assertion that succession through the female line occurred in all cases of doubt, but the case for matrilineal succession remains intact.

By the early 630s Ciniod was over-king of Pictavia, and his reign witnessed important changes in Pictland. The first of these was the continuing exile of his competitors. One Eanfrith remained in exile for many years. Some spent their years of exile in Scottish Dalriada, where they were baptised by the priests of Columba's Gaelic church. Their baptism took place on Iona and placed them under the spiritual influence of its abbot. But there is no sign of hostilities between the Scots and the Picts at this time, and the Picts looked to Iona for leadership in Catholic matters and for ecclesiastical assistance in spiritual affairs.

A number of entries in the annals show the Scots becoming involved in Irish wars, but the Picts seem to have enjoyed a period of relative peace in the early seventh century. Their neighbours in the west were preoccupied with Ireland, while in the south Edwin warred mostly in Wales and the English Midlands. There were two changes affecting the pattern of power in the North at the end of Ciniod's reign, the first being the accession in 631 of Domnall Brecc to the kingship of Cenel nGabrain, who contested the throne of Dalriada. The second key event at the close of Ciniod's reign came in 633 – perhaps the year of his death. At a battle Edwin was beaten and killed, the victor being Cadwallon,

King of the Britons of North Wales.

Now those who had been exiled returned, and the ruling parties of Pictavia claimed their birthright. Pictavia was now turned into a pagan state, for the King of Pictavia renounced the Christianity he had been converted to in exile. At the same time, a cousin of Edwin was slain in battle, and in the wake of this the Welsh king unleashed a terrible fury on the northern English, with great slaughter of the native population. There were assassinations at high level. The Picts no doubt wondered how events would go, but Pictavia did not take sides in the quarrels of her southern neighbours.

The Picts may now have feared an onslaught on their kingdom by the sword of Cadwallon; but all this changed in the following year, 634, when the sons of potentates returned from exile to claim their heritage. The King of Cenel nGabrain sent a military force to assist in the dislodging of Cadwallon. The Welsh king was brought into battle at Hexham, near Hadrian's Wall, his war bands being defeated while he himself fled from the battlefield. At length Cadwallon was cut down by the English swords.

Now a Christian king came to the fore, whose loyalty lay with the abbots in the North and not with the Archbishop of Canterbury.

The Christian King Oswald summoned monks from Iona to convert his heathen subjects; the island of Lindisfarne, off the Northumbrian coast, was given to the missionaries as a base. Oswald's departure from Kintyre to fight Cadwallon would have been possible without the blessing of Domnall Brecc. With Oswald's family now installed in Bernicia, the descendants of nGabrain now had a useful friend on the borders of their territory. In Pictavia its kings were now relieved that Bernicia was now ruled by a king who shared a

Gaelic Christian faith and whose older sibling had fathered their own royal prince, Talorcan.

There is no evidence that Oswald changed his friendly relations with the Scots and Picts. Bede asserts that he eventually held all the northern people under his dominion, but this is hard to believe and it is perhaps wishful thinking. He says that Oswald's hegemony may not have reached into Pictavia or Argyll. The extent of English rule in the North was in fact unknown before the reign of Oswiu, the successor and younger brother of Oswald. Bede states that he was the first English king to attain a large overlordship. Neither the *Ecclesiastical History of the English People* nor the Irish annals records any military campaigns by Oswald against the Scots or Picts. But one campaign by Oswald had profound implications for the Picts. This was the English conquest of the Lothians, who were ruled from Edinburgh Castle Rock. At this time Edinburgh was known as Din Eidyn.

The siege of Edinburgh in 640 marked a crucial moment in Northumbria's expansion. Few people in Pictavia and Dalriada would have mourned the demise of the Gododdin kings, who had a long hostility to Picts and Scots. In late Roman times the Votandi had functioned as a buffer state between Roman Britain and Pictavia in the frontier districts near the Antonine earth wall. Many in Pictavia rejoiced at the defeat of the enemy. Others may have felt less assured by the coming of war bands to the shores of the Firth of Forth.

At this time the Picts were ruled by three successive over-kings, but there is little known about them except the dates of their deaths. Brude, who died in 641, was ruling Pictavia in 640 when a Dalriada army led an attack upon an unknown area recorded in the Irish annals. The battle occurred in the same year as the siege of Etin, said to have taken place in the

Loch Ness region, not far from the border between the Scots and the Picts. The battle marked the end of a long period of peaceful relations between the Scots and the Picts.

Domnall Brecc of Dalriada battle fame is recorded as having fought many battles in Ireland and Argyll, but he suffered a number of defeats. If his enemies were Picts, the victor was perhaps Brude, son of Gwid. Oswald's main enemy lay to the south, in Mercia, where ruled a mighty expanding state under a warlord called Penda, and he now challenged Penda for the overlordship of southern and Midland Britain.

In August 642, perhaps in Shropshire, Oswald was defeated in a great battle against the Mercian king and his many allies. Here Oswald was killed, his corpse being dismembered and displayed on stakes. His kingdom now splintered into two parts. At the same time his dynasty of Deira reasserted itself, but it fell under the sway of Penda, who was now the most powerful ruler in Britain.

In December of the following year Domnall Brecc died in a battle against the Britons of Alt Clut. The Britons were led by their king, whose defeat of the Scots made him the strongest ruler in the North and a potential rival of Penda. The *Historia Brittonum* records that the riches yielded by Oswiu were distributed by Penda among the kings of the Britons.

Indew is usually identified with the ancient fortress at Stirling, known to Bede as Urbs Giudi in the Dark Ages or early historic period, the stronghold of high-status rulers. The fortress was probably utilized by the Mercian kings as suitable for their dealings with Oswiu, having fled north to make themselves overlords of the area. Bede provides a different version of the turn of events, saying that money paid in ransom affected Penda, but here we may accept the

Historia Brittonum as a more accurate record. Although the Picts played no part in these disagreements, they no doubt were concerned about hostile neighbours who wanted to invade their kingdom. As far as it is known, Oswiu had little contact with Pictavia and was not in a position to seek Pictish aid in his war of survival. His nephew Talorcan was in every way a Pict, and may have had little in common with his English uncle.

The kings of these areas were commoners by blood. This fits well into the theory of matrilineal succession, in which royal power was regularly inherited by the son of a king's sister. The lack of any record of hostile relations between Pictavia, Penda and Mercia at this time further suggests that policies of non-interference were the rule in regard to relations with Penda. Had the Picts chosen to join the Britons as Penda's military allies the two kingdoms of Northumbria would almost certainly have been crushed and their royal dynasties exiled. Talorcan accordingly in 653 placed a half-English king over the Picts, but this was not necessarily helpful for Oswiu. Some historians think that Talorcan was a puppet imposed on Pictavia by his Bernician uncle, but this is not likely.

Oswiu was an ambitious king who hoped to regain the paramount status formally enjoyed by Oswald and Aethelfrith, but in 653 his capacity for intervention in the North, or anywhere else, was hindered by the continuing menace of Penda. Oswiu now mustered an army for a power struggle with Oswine, the king of Deira, but his primary concern was the dark shadow cast by the Mercian ruler. During his childhood exile on Iona his family had carried on peaceful relations with Cenel nGabrain for many years. If he had any political influence over Talorcan, the conflict at Strathyre, which saw the death of the nGabrain prince, should never have happened. Both nephew and uncle may have been openly hostile to one another.

The situation again changed when in 665 Penda was defeated in a battle near Leeds. The Mercian king died, leaving the Bernician as conqueror of Deira and over-king of all Northumbria. Bede states that Oswiu subjected the greater part of Pictavia to his rule, but he does not state how this was accomplished. Bede's reports of Oswiu's subjection of large parts of Pictish territory might be an exaggeration. In reality the English overlordship probably did not reach as far as the River Tay, although some part of Pictavia fell under Oswiu's direct control. A bishopric was set up at Abercorn, on the southern shore of the Firth of Forth. Abercorn was an ecclesiastical authority over the Picts founded as late as 681. It was during this period that an expedition was made by Cuthbert, who later became Bishop of Lindisfarne and Northumbria's patron saint. With a small number of companions he set sail, intending to reach a part of Pictavia inhabited by a people called Niduaria, but bad weather was encountered and provisions started to fall low. However, they were able to eat dolphin meat. The storm lasted for three days.

Talorcan's successor as a paramount ruler of the Picts was Gartnait, who reigned from 657 to 663. Battles followed in 664, but the battle sites cannot be identified. The Irish annals site one of the battles at Lutho-feitinn. The year of this battle saw a huge significance for Scotland's religious history, and the repercussions were felt across parts of northern Britain. The Synod of Whitby, a gathering of prominent churchmen, was convened by Oswiu at the Northumbrian monastery of Whitby.

The synod's main purpose was to iron out the differences between the Roman clergy and the Celtic or Gaelic ones. Its leading figures acknowledged the authority of the Pope, but Scotland was remote from Roman influence in the way of religion, along with the Gaelic church in Ireland. Celtic monks, for instance, were tonsured not according to the Roman fashion, but by shaving the front of the scalp from ear to ear; the Roman method left a crown of hair encircling the shaven scalp. But by far the most important difference between the two rites was the calculation of the date of Easter. As a result of this, Easter Sunday on Iona did not always coincide with Easter Sunday in Rome. Matters came to a head in the seventh century, partly because both traditions were practised among the northern English. Bernicia, for example, had been evangelized by priests of the Gaelic church invited from Iona by King Oswald. Monasteries like Whitby came under Iona and were bastions of Gaelic or Celtic Christianity; they formed part of the Columban church, whose influence had spread across northern Britain.

Southern Britain was now evangelized by St Augustine, who came from Rome in 597. Augustine became the first Archbishop of Canterbury.

At the time of the Synod of Whitby the churches of Pictavia lay securely under Iona and were answerable to its abbot. The extent of Iona's influence among the Picts in the seventh century can be seen in the place names and church dedications commemorating its principal figures, such as the men that followed Columba in the abbacy. The abbots were usually Irishmen of noble background, and often hailed from powerful families closely related to Columba's own kin.

Wells in Pictavia were named after Fergan, who held the abbacy as a Briton from 605 to 623. The close proximity of a holy well and ancient church suggests the focus of an early cult devoted to this little-known saint. Fergan's sister was the mother of an Ionian priest to whom the Perthshire church of Rossie was dedicated. It was later rededicated, in 1243, by the Bishop of St Andrews. Iona's seventh abbot was Cummene the White, who wrote a life of Columba that preceded that of Adomnan, but it has not survived. Cummene is commemorated in several areas of Pictavia, in places where conversions were made.

It was during Cummene's abbacy that the Synod of Whitby convened to debate the future of Iona in Northumbrian church affairs. This great gathering of churchmen featured many important names from both the Roman and Celtic traditions. The proceedings were chaired by the Abbess of Whitby, herself a prominent figure in the Columban church in Northumbria. Bede has given us information about the proceedings to decide whether the British church would fall under Iona or Canterbury. This seems not to have affected the Pictavia church, but the Synod of Whitby had profound long-term consequences that changed the ecclesiastical map of Britain, limiting Iona's influence to Pictavia, without any foothold south of the Forth–Clyde line. The Clyde Britons still adhered to Celtic Christianity, but the bishops had never come under Iona's sway.

Sometime during the reign of the Pictish over-king Brust, the remaining Picts of the Western Isles became locked in conflict with their Dalriada enemies. The precise circumstances are not clear, but, according to the Irish Gaelic annals, hostilities broke out on the Isle of Skye in the late 660s. In one entry the annalist noted the voyage of the sons of Gartnait to Ireland, with the people of Skye. The second entry relates to 670 and states that the people of Gartnait came from Ireland, where they spent two years in Eirinn. Nothing is said of what was happening on Skye at this time. A tale shows that one Cano and his father as members of a high-status family on Skye were oppressed by Aeden mac Gabrain. After Gartnait's death Cano fled to Ireland, where he fell in love with Cred, who had Dalriada origins, but his name suggests Pictish ancestry. Perhaps he was a man of mixed blood, descended from the Picts. Cano also bore a non-Gaelic name, which may have been Pictish.

The Tale of Cano is awry in its portrayal of Aedan as the enemy of a principal hero. In the Irish annals the activities of Cano and Garnait occurred long after Aedan's death in 608. The slaying of Cano is reported in 687. The final entry refers to the killing of one Conamail in 673. The most that can be said is that the tale contains a kernel of truth wrapped in layers of legend. Its hero was evidently a real figure in seventh-century history whose career was summarized by the annalists. From the latter it can be deduced that Cano was a local ruler of Skye who travelled to Ireland in 668 before returning home to die in 687.

Skye was finally conquered by Pictish or non-Pictish rulers. If the annals are correct the struggle for Skye was a protracted war spanning half a century. At the same time Drust was still reigning over the Picts when Oswiu died in 670. He was the only king in seventh-century Northumbria not to have died in battle, instead having a peaceful end. His son Ecgfrith, then a young man in his twenties, laid claim to the wider hegemony that had been established by Oswald and Oswiu, including the territories in the English Pennines that had formerly come under native British kings. Northumbria had conquered these kings, extinguishing their power and expelling them from their lands. The Britons that had established themselves in Cumbria and Lancashire acknowledged Ecgfrith's overlordship at his accession in 670; there is no record of revolt by whatever remained of the native aristocracy.

The situation further north was different. Oswiu's supremacy over his neighbours in Pictavia, Dalriada and the Clyde had been sustained by military might. His heir, Ecgfrith, ascended the throne as a novice who had proven himself to be a man of strength and ruthless ambition. If he failed to rule the empire created by his father, a Pict, Scot or Briton might claim the overlordship of the North. It would only be a matter of time until his mettle would be put to the test.

Now a portion of Pictavia rose in rebellion, perhaps at the instigation of Drust, the Pictish over-king. Ecgfrith had no intention of relinquishing his father's gains, so he attacked the rebels. The following campaign was reported by Stephen of Ripon, an English monk writing in the eighth century. He called the Picts a 'bestial people'. King Drust hoped to free the conquered Picts' territory from English rule. Ecgfrith hurried north leading an army of mounted warriors, and their rapid advance brought him face-to-face with the enemy; however, the English won the day. According to Stephen, the Picts killed a great number of people, filling two rivers with bodies of the slain. The victory confirmed Ecgfrith in his father's gains and ensured that the southern Pictish elites continued to make tribute payments to Northumbria.

Around the same time as Ecgfrith's victory, Drust was expelled from Pictland by unidentified opponents for reasons unknown. The Irish annals noted the event in 672, in the early years of Ecgfrith's reign. Some sources say that Drust was ousted by internal rivals, who deemed him unworthy of kingship after Ecgfrith's victory. Those that regarded Drust as a Northumbrian vassal place his expulsion before the battle, but the precise circumstances will perhaps never be known. He was succeeded by Prode, a man who was to become the most famous Pictish king of the seventh century.

CHAPTER TWO

In the final quarter of the seventh century a unified Northumbria was the most powerful kingdom in Britain. In the person of Ecgfrith it possessed an energetic king determined to build upon the successes of his predecessors. Brude was one of the kings that paid tribute to Ecgfrith, involving regular offerings of livestock, agricultural produce and other material resources; he also had to provide hospitality to the foreign overlord tribute collectors.

For Brude and other northern kings, the key moment arrived in 679 when Ecgfrith fought a great battle against the Mercians near the River Trent. But the outcome was not decisive, so both sides were itching to resume hostilities. Ecgfrith emerged as the loser after the Church intervened to alleviate the tension. His enemy in the battle was Aethelfred, whose objective was to win back the Mercian province of Lindsey from Northumbrian control. The objective was achieved and the Archbishop of Canterbury negotiated terms of peace. The treaty left Ecgfrith's hegemony diminished, his domain and his political ambitions in the south reduced. Now the vassal kings around the Forth–Clyde began to rise up against him. The main challenge would come from the Picts, whose recent revolt Ecgfrith had crushed in 672. Under the strong leadership of Brude, the Picts were once again a formidable people. By 679 the aristocracy were longing to take up the sword and to reassert their independence.

Brude wanted to stop paying tribute to Northumbria, and this led him to have a showdown with Ecgfrith. The growing tension between these two kings led to an ecclesiastical intervention by the Archbishop of Canterbury, who now set about redrawing the ecclesiastical map of England. In 681 the Archbishop broke the Bernician see into three parts, establishing new bishoprics. This gave Ecgfrith's subjection of the Picts an aura of permanence as it implied that it was the will of God.

It was at this time that Brude began to flex his muscles in the outlying areas of his kingdom. The annals mention a siege of Sunnottar in 681. This fort lay by the coast near the present town of Stonehaven, a few miles south of Aberdeen. In the late seventh century this fort was perhaps the residence of a wavering lord who needed to be reminded of his obligations to Brude of Pictavia. Brude won the encounter, and he now launched an attack against Orkney, for Brude regarded that too as part of his empire. He demanded hostages from the Orcadians and imposed his will upon them by force of arms.

In the following year he besieged another outpost at the hillfort of Dundurn, whose geographical situation was stategically important. Bringing Dundurn to heel consolidated Brude's position within his realm, and now much tribute was to be paid to him. During this period of aggression Brude undertook a series of military strikes to stamp his authority on outlying areas of Pictavia.

Ecgfrith, meanwhile, was nursing wounded pride after the frustration of his northern ambitions, but he was soon itching for another contest with Mercia. In 684, five years after the Battle of Trent, he once more sent his soldiers to war. His aggression was directed not only against Mercia, but also against the Irish Midlands.

The motive behind these campaigns is not clear, although a number of theories have been proposed. One theory suggests that Ecgfrith sought to deter Irish support for his half-brother, the illegitimate child of the Ui Neill dynasty of the High Kings of Eirinn; but according to Bede, Ecgfrith and his siblings did not regard their half-brother as a potential rival at all. Another possible motive for the attack is found in the Irish *Annals of Clonmacnoise*, which refers to an alliance between the Irish and the Britons. If such an alliance ever existed in the 680s, then a punitive raid upon Ireland could have made sense. A further motive has a religious dimension: Ecgfrith, with the Pope's blessing, pursued the interests of the Roman Catholic Church by terrorizing a country where the priests still held spiritual sway. The sources do not offer any theories of their own, and thus it is hard to understand why the attacks happened at all.

The influential churchman Ecgbert warned against the raids and said that the Irish had done no harm to Northumbria, but his warning went unheeded. The venture was a failure and damaged Ecgfrith's reputation at home and abroad.

The Scots army invaded Ireland and rampaged across the Plain of Brega – an area that includes the ancient royal site of Tara and other hallowed places. The English warriors attacked churches and monasteries with great ferocity, shocking observers on either side of the Irish Sea.

The invaders returned to their ships laden with many captives, who were taken back to Northumbria as hostages. Even Bede, who was a boy at the time, wrote later of the wickedness of the campaign in Ireland and counted it among one of Ecgfrith's worst sins. On 26 March of the same year, on Easter Sunday, Ecgfrith and his chief clergy assembled at York to witness the consecration of Cuthbert as Bishop of Lindisfarne, headed by the Archbishop of Canterbury, who urged Ecgfrith not to seek a showdown with Brude. Four weeks later, on 23 April, Ecgfrith visited the monastery of Jarrow, beside the River Trent. The dedication stone, bearing the date and the King's name, can still be seen in situ in the wall. Soon afterwards the Northumbrian army marched against the Picts.

Ecgfrith's route probably followed the old Roman road known as the Deira Road, which ran along the eastern side of his kingdom from the Tyne to the Firth of Forth. The road was bereft of traffic for about 300 years, but it was still functional. It followed a direct course through Lothian to reach the long-disused Roman fort of Cramond. From there the Northumbrian army would have continued northward to cross the River Forth at what is now Stirling Castle Rock. To the east lay Fife; to the north lay the rivers Larne and Tay, and here the Northumbrian army crossed via fords in the shadow of the Pictish fortress on Moncrieff Hill.

The invaders now marched into southern Pictavia, plundering the rich agricultural lands, which enabled the confiscation of food for the army while ensuring that the same resources were unavailable to Brude. Swampy terrain to the east forced Ecgfrith to follow the course of the Tay upstream to its junction with the River Isla; from here he turned north-east along the great Vale of Strathmore, taking a route followed by the modern road from Perth to Forfar.

In 685 part of Strathmore was a dangerous landscape of bogs, lakes and pools, which would have been difficult to traverse for a large body of warriors marching in unfamiliar territory.

Now Ecgfrith led his troops over firmer terrain on the northern side of the Dean Water. The invading army would now be led into a trap, being drawn deeper into Pictish territory. On 20 May, at about three o'clock in the afternoon, the army of Ecgfrith clashed in a great battle with the Picts. Bede has reported the event, but does not give its location; he wrote that the fighting took place in narrow passes in the midst of deep mountains. The Irish annalists called the battlefield Dun Nechtain – a name of Gaelic rather than Pictish origin; the Picts' name for the place is unknown, but later Welsh texts called it Linn Garan (Crane Lake). Since the Picts spoke a tongue similar to Brittonic, they too may have called it Linn Garan, or something similar.

The battle was basically a clash of foot soldiers, with limited fighting on horseback. Cavalry warfare was not common in the British Isles during this period. Horses were valued as high-status possessions, and their main military use was to transport soldiers to the battlefield. There the riders dismounted, leaving their horses in the care of weaponless servants while they themselves fought on foot, so battles were a melee of infantry versus infantry. Swords, spears, axes and shields were the tools of their trade, but there was not much archery. Graves have been unearthed which show the terrible injuries inflicted by bladed weapons.

The encounter at Nechtanesmere in 685 would have been a scene of bloody savagery. Its outcome was a great victory for the Picts, for Ecgfrith and most of his army were killed; his loyal bodyguard of chosen warriors fought to the last man, until all were slain around him.

Historians generally agree that the Dun Nechtain of the

Irish annals was an ancient fortification on Dunnichen Hill near Forfar. The broken remnants of a wall were visible in the eighteenth century, but much of the stonework was removed for other building purposes by local people. Near here there is a small pond – all that remains of a large expanse of water which lay in the shadow of Dun Nechtain. In recent years this view has been challenged – the site of Brude's victory over his enemies may be elsewhere. In order to reach the battlefield the Northumbrian warriors would have had to traverse the southern slopes of the hill and negotiate the expanse of the loch, with its swamps, or perhaps the Northumbrian army crossed Strathmore at the head of Loch Forfar before marching along the south side of Restenneth Loch to confront Brude's army below the northern slopes of Dunnichen Hill. But other sites have been suggested.

Bede was not, however, an eyewitness to the event, and he had to rely on recycled information of the kind available to historians who study the battle today. Bede's main purpose was not to give a precise description of the battlefield topography, but to show Ecgfrith being trapped and slain by the Picts as a divine punishment for his assault on the monasteries of Ireland.

It is curious that the Welsh and English sources associate the battle with a lake or mere, whereas the Irish annals suggest a hill or hillfort as the key topographical feature. It is likely that the main part of the combat took place on the strip of land which once lay between the waters of the loch and the lower slopes of the hill.

On the day of the battle, St Cuthbert was visiting Carlisle, where Queen Iurmingberg, Ecgfrith's second wife, sat waiting anxiously in a nunnery where her sister governed as abbess. During the afternoon the royal official gave Cuthbert a tour of the local Roman antiquities. He was shown a finely carved fountain, but he became agitated and looked towards the sky. Something led him to believe that the war was ended, but the victory was against Ecgfrith's warriors.

One of the few survivors of Ecgfrith's army reached Carlisle to bring news of the Pictish victory and to inform the Queen that her husband had died. Contemporary writers in Northumbria described the battle as wretched and mournful and a great disaster. For Bede it marked a turning point in Northumbria's fortunes. He wrote that the hopes of the English kingdom had ebbed away, and remarked that the Picts had recovered their own land, which the English had formerly held. The Scots in Dalriada also threw off the Northumbrian yoke to recover their independence. In political terms this meant that the King of Pictavia, Dalriada and Alt Clut shook off the burden of paying tribute to an English overlord.

Around the Firth of Forth, Northumbrian families found their situation untenable in the face of the Picts. A terrible fate awaited them as Brude's Pictish army stormed across the Tay to reclaim the conquered lands. Bede wrote that many in the region had been slain by the sword or enslaved in Pictish territory. The most high-profile refugee was the Bishop of Abercorn, who fled with his monks to seek sanctuary in the monastery of Whitby, where he ended his days, never returning to his homeland. As for Ecgfrith, he was put to death by the Pictish warriors. His body was sent to Iona for burial – a wish of Brude. Ecgfrith's widow may have wanted Ecgfrith to be buried somewhere in his native Northumbria, but the decision was not hers to make.

Aelfflaed, Ecgfrith's sister, jointly governed the monastery of Whitby with her mother.

For Brude, the most immediate consequence was that

he no longer was obliged to send tribute payments to Northumbria. The tribute paid to Northumbria would now fall into the purse of Brude. He now brought the outlying lands of Pictavia more firmly under his control, laying the foundations of the great kingdom that would eventually rise to power in the following century.

It is more difficult to assess the political gains of the Battle of Dunnichen. It did not, as some historians believe, prevent an imminent English conquest of the entire Pictish nation, for such a venture would have lain beyond Ecgfrith's wide ambitions. Nor did it extinguish Northumbria's territorial claims around the Firth of Forth.

The Kingdom of Bernicia would produce no great warrior kings in the following generation because it was a period of dynastic instability, but in political terms Northumbria would remain a powerful force and would continue to play an important role in Pictish affairs for some years to come.

Brude's victory became a famous event in Scottish history, ranking with Bannockburn, Flodden and Culloden. However, there is a lack of information on the matter, so it cannot be elevated to the others' lofty heights. But to Bede it was a decisive battle, and to his contemporaries in Pictavia it must have seemed equally important.

There is a lack of written evidence about it, but some modern observers believe that Brude's triumph was immortalized in stone by skilled artisans. The stone is an upright slab, seven feet high, standing today in the kirkyard at Aberlemno Hill among the reed-grown meadows where Restenneth Loch formerly lay. The stone is one of several monuments in the region of Aberlemno, but it is by far the most striking of the group. On one side is carved a cross of intricate workmanship; on the other side there are Pictish symbols at the top. Beneath this are images of warriors engaged in battle. The upper section shows two horsemen, one pursuing the other. The fleeing horseman sports a helmet with a nose guard, while his pursuer is long-haired and brandishes a sword. Infantrymen are also recorded, and horsemen face each other in combat while a helmeted warrior on foot is devoured by a raven.

The precise date of this monument is unknown, but the style is of the eighth century. The helmets depicted are similar in design to the Coppergate Helmet, a striking eighth-century Northumbrian artefact recovered during excavations at York. There are, however, major difficulties in believing this stone to be a commemoration of the battle, for it is claimed that the carvings were made no earlier than the eighth century. The date assigned to the carvings places them around the middle of the century, two generations after Brude's victory. Doubts have also arisen about the style of the clothing worn by the English warriors: archaeologists do not believe that helmets of the Coppergate type were available in seventh-century Northumbria.

In every major aspect of its artistic and archaeological contexts the monument seems to commemorate an event of the eighth century rather than of the seventh or the ninth. Possible alternative battles from the decades after 700 do in fact exist, most notably in the campaigns of the Pictish King Oengus, son of Fergus, against Dalriada and Alt Clut between 734 and 756. It is possible that scenes inspired by one of Oengus's battles were carved on the monument in the kirkyard at Aberlemno.

A quite different memorial in the form of a poem was written to commemorate Brude's victory at the Battle of Dunnichen, but only a portion survives. The lines are attributed to an

Irish priest called Riaguil, who lived among the Picts at the time of the battle, but the poet is more likely to be a Pictish bard whose name is now forgotten. Bards were important members of a king's entourage, for they proclaimed their patron's fame and status at ceremonial gatherings; they praised the king's past deeds, forming a kind of ancient public-relations exercise.

The mention of 'blue swords' in the poem may be a reference to oxidization resulting from reheating iron blades to make them stronger, unless it refers to the bluish hue of steel. The 'black draughts' associated with Ecgfrith's death are the deep gaping wounds from which he died on the battlefield.

More intriguing is the claim that Brude fought for the heritage of his grandfather, which implies that the Pictish king's ancestry gave him an additional motive or objective. The poet does not state which grandfather he is referring to. No source names Brude's mother, but as she gave birth to a Pictish king she is likely to have been a lady of Pictish royal blood.

Some of the territory disputed was that menaced by the Northumbrian army on the day of the battle. Perhaps this area had once belonged to Brude's maternal grandfather – the patriarch of a family in which the male children were groomed as potential over-kings of Pictavia. This family may have ruled the lands around Dunnichen Hill as the Lords of Circinn, an ancient province which is now in the county of Angus.

In 830 the Welsh author of the *Historia Brittonum* presented his own comments on the Northumbrian defeat, writing that Ecgfrith had perished along with the best of his army and that the Picts with their over-king were defeated.

His information was based on Bede, but it contains curious references about a blood relationship between the two kings. Central to the debate is the Welsh author's use of the Latin term *fratrulis*, which had a fairly precise meaning denoting male cousins who were the sons of siblings; but opinion is divided about who these siblings were, male or female. Various theories have been put forward to explain this relationship between Ecgfrith and Brude. Some of these theories are based on Brude's connection with the Pictish King Talorcan, whose father was related to Ecgfrith, but such a connection is unlikely. Some think that Brude had no Pictish parents at all. All that can be said is that the author of the *Historia Brittonum* saw nothing improbable in the idea that Brude and Ecgfrith were cousins in some way, even if their kinship was once or twice removed.

Brude died in 693, ending his life peacefully rather than in battle. His remains were brought to Iona, where an all-night vigil was held. Legend has it that his body showed signs of life. One source states that Adomnan grieved beside the corpse before blessing Brude's soul. He criticized the humble burial of the over-king, for Brude's body was placed in an ordinary wooden coffin.

Brude was laid to rest in the monastic graveyard on Iona. This hallowed site, which also held the bones of Ecgfrith, now became the final resting place of the proud victor of Dun Nechtain. Within eight years of the great clash of arms these two mighty kings were reunited in peace on the Holy Island of Iona, of Columba fame.

SELECT BIBLIOGRAPHY

Forsyth, K., *Language in Pictland* (Utreacht, 1997).

Nicolaisen, W. F. H., *The Picts and Their Place Names* (Rosemarkie, 1996).

Rivet, A. L. F., and Smith, C., *The Place Names of Roman Britain* (London, 1981).

Watson, W. J., *The History of Celtic Place Names of Scotland* (Edinburgh, 1926).